Cornelius

GURLITT

THE FIRST LESSONS

Opus 117

FOR PIANO

K 03498

The First Lessons.
Die Anfangs-Stunden.

C. GURLITT. Op. 117.

Moderato. 112

1.

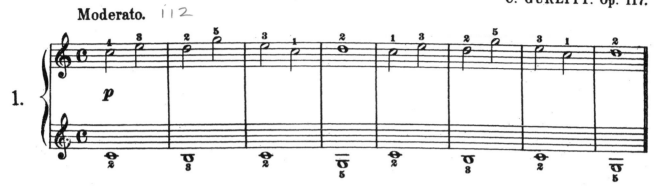

Moderato.

2.

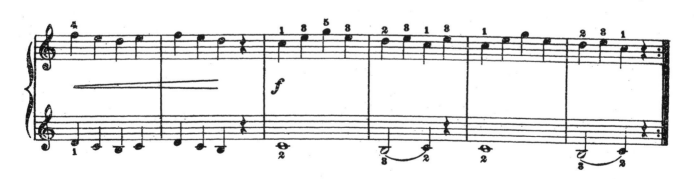

Printed in the U. S. A.

Moderato.

7.

p scherzando.

Vivace.

8.

f risoluto.

Allegretto.

11.

Moderato.

12.

Morning Salute.
Morgengruss.

Going to School.
Zur Schule.

8

The Chase.
Die Jagd.

15.

Lamentation.
Klage.

Cradle Song.
Wiegenliedchen.

10

The little Rogue.
Der kleine Schelm.

18.

The good Child.
Das artige Kind.

19.

Even-Song.
Abendliedchen.

20. Andantino.

Catch me.
Das Häschen.

21. Con moto.

Round.
Reigen.

The Departure.
Abschied.

The Return.
Wiedersehen.

Cornelius Gurlitt. Op. 117, № 24.

The brave Soldier.
Der tapfere Soldat.

Moderato, tempo di Marcia.

25.

The little Savoyard.
Der kleine Savojarde.

Con moto.

26.

Hymn.
Hymne.

27.

The poor Child.
Das arme Kind.

Merry Company.
Lustige Gesellschaft.

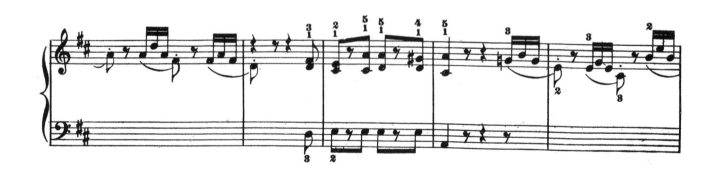

The Hobby Horse.
Das Steckenpferd.

Con moto.

30.

Gavotte.

31.

The hardy Horseman.
Der kühne Reiter.

Clappermill.
Die Klappermühle.

Song without Words.
Lied ohne Worte.

Allegretto.

34.